Fitness and wellness made simple:

A No-Fluff Beginning

By
Giane Lollar

Copyright © 2025 by Giane Lollar

All rights reserved. This book or any portion thereof may not be reproduced or used in any manner whatsoever without the express written permission of the publisher, except for the use of brief quotations in a book review.

Contents

Introduction vi
   Why Simple Works vi
   Chapter 1 Understanding Fitness and Wellness 1
   The Four Pillars of Fitness 1
   The Other Half: Wellness 2
   The Connection 2
   Keep It Simple 3

Chapter 2 4
Why You Should Start Today 4
   The Real Reason to Start 4
   The Power of Momentum 5
   Excuses vs. Progress 6
   The Gift of Movement 7
   Start Simple, Start Now 7

Chapter 3 When to Train: Building Your Routine 9
   Morning Training 9
   Evening Training 10
   Consistency Beats Timing 11
   Building a Weekly Routine 11
   Rest Is Part of Training 12
   Your Time, Your Rules 12

Chapter 4 14
Where to Start: Movement Basics 14

The Five Basic Movements 14

How to Start 15

Beginner Full-Body Routine (3x per week): 16

Progress Over Perfection 16

Keep It Safe 17

The Takeaway 17

Chapter 5 Staying Consistent: The Real Secret 19

Why Consistency Matters 19

Build the Habit 20

Tips to stay on track: 20

Progress Over Perfection 21

Progress looks like: 21

When Life Gets in the Way 21

The Takeaway 22

Chapter 6 Mindset & Motivation: Training the Inner Game . 23

Why Mindset Matters 23

Motivation vs. Discipline 24

How to stay driven: 24

Train Your Mind Like You Train Your Body 25

The Power of Patience 25

The Takeaway 26

Chapter 7 Staying in the Game: Longevity & Lifestyle 27

Think Long-Term 27

Build Habits, Not Phases 28
Focus on these fundamentals: 28
Adapt as You Grow 28
Keep Learning 29
The Takeaway 30
Conclusion: Keep It Simple, Keep Going **31**

*Life is as simple as these three questions:
What do I want? Why do I want it?
And how will I achieve it?*
-Shannon L Adler

Introduction

Starting your fitness journey can feel **overwhelming**. There is endless advice online, conflicting information, and countless voices claiming to have the "secret." However, the truth is that fitness is not complicated. It is about simple, small, consistent actions that add up over time.

This guide was written to make things **simple**. No fluff. No gimmicks. Just clear, practical information to help you understand what to do, why it matters, and how to stay consistent.

You do not need to be an athlete, a gym enthusiast, or someone with fancy equipment. All you need is the willingness to start, to learn, and to keep showing up.

Inside these pages, you will learn how to move better, eat smarter, build discipline, and create a healthy lifestyle that lasts. Whether your goal is to lose weight, gain strength, or simply feel better in your body, this is your foundation.

This is not about perfection; it is about progress. Real change happens gradually, through small choices repeated daily. The transformation you seek is not found in extreme measures or crash diets. It is found in sustainable habits that become part of who you are. You will discover that fitness is not something you do for a few months; it is something you become. And that journey starts with understanding that you are capable of more than you think.

Why Simple Works

There is considerable noise in the fitness and **wellness** space. Everyone is selling shortcuts, 30-day transformations, and complicated meal plans that sound like science experiments. The truth is that none of that lasts. Real fitness is about discipline, consistency, and keeping things simple enough to sustain.

That is what this book is about: cutting through the fluff.

You do not need to know every detail about macronutrients or memorize every muscle in the body to start getting healthy. You just need to understand what to do, why it matters, and how to keep doing it one workout, one meal, one day at a time.

Fitness and wellness are connected. It is not just about lifting weights or losing pounds. It is about feeling stronger, thinking more clearly, moving with purpose, and showing up for yourself every single day. When your body is strong, your mind follows. When your mind is focused, your body performs at a higher level. They feed each other.

This guide was made for beginners: people who want to start but do not know where to begin, and people who are tired of confusion and want real results without the nonsense. Whether you have never stepped foot in a gym or you are getting back on track after time away, this is your foundation. You will learn the what, why, when, and how of fitness and wellness, broken down simply and clearly.

I am not here to overcomplicate things or impress you with fancy terminology. I am here to help you build discipline, develop strength, and improve your health for life.

If you commit to this process and apply what is in these pages, you will realize that being fit is not reserved for athletes or entertainers. It is for anyone willing to put in the work. The fitness industry profits from complexity, from making you feel like you need special programs, expensive supplements, or exclusive knowledge. You do not.

What you need is clarity, commitment, and the courage to start where you are. Simple beats complicated every single time because simple is what you can maintain. And what you can maintain is what transforms your life.

No fluff. No gimmicks. Just results.

Welcome to Fitness and Wellness Made Simple.

Chapter 1
Understanding Fitness and Wellness

Fitness and wellness are often misunderstood concepts. When most people hear the word "fitness," they immediately think of abs, weights, or treadmills. However, true fitness goes deeper than physical appearance.

Fitness is your body's ability to move, work, and recover effectively. It is about having the strength and endurance to handle whatever life throws at you, whether that is lifting groceries, playing with your children, or finishing a long day without feeling drained.

The Four Pillars of Fitness

Fitness is composed of four essential pillars:

- **Strength:** Your ability to move resistance
- **Endurance:** How long you can sustain physical activity
- **Flexibility:** How freely your joints and muscles move
- **Balance:** Your stability and control during movement

You do not need to master all of these at once. Simply aim to improve a little in each area over time. Small progress accumulates quickly.

These pillars are like the foundation of a house. If one is weak, the entire structure suffers. An athlete with great strength but poor flexibility will eventually face injury. Someone with excellent endurance but no balance will struggle with coordination.

The Other Half: Wellness

If fitness trains your body, wellness trains your life. Wellness includes everything that supports your physical work: sleep, nutrition, stress management, and mindset. You can train six days a week, but if you eat poorly, stay up late, or carry heavy stress, your results will stall.

Wellness means taking care of yourself beyond the gym, mentally, spiritually, and emotionally.

- Get enough rest
- Eat food that gives you energy instead of draining it
- Take quiet time when you need it
- Surround yourself with people who support your goals

When your mind is right, your body follows.

Wellness is the invisible work that makes visible results possible. The quality of your sleep determines how well you recover. Nutritious meals that fuel your workouts. Stress management prevents burnout.

The Connection

Fitness and wellness feed each other. Training builds strength and confidence, while wellness keeps you fueled and focused. Skip either one, and you will burn out. Combine them, and you will thrive.

Here is the simple **formula**: Move your body, fuel it right, rest well, repeat.

That is fitness and wellness in one sentence. It does not need to be fancy; it just needs to be consistent.

Keep It Simple

You do not have to live in the gym or eat a perfect diet to be healthy. Start with small wins:

- Walk 15 minutes a day
- Do bodyweight movements a few times a week
- Drink water instead of soda
- Go to bed earlier

Over time, these basics will change how you look, move, and feel.

Fitness and wellness are not separate goals. They are two sides of the same coin, both built on discipline, patience, and daily effort. Once you understand that, you will realize how simple this can be. The power of simplicity is that it removes barriers. When you strip away the complexity, you are left with actions you can actually sustain. And sustainability is what creates lasting change.

Chapter 2
Why You Should Start Today

There is never a perfect time to start your fitness journey. People wait for the "right" schedule, the "right" energy, or the "right" motivation, but those things rarely appear on their own.

The truth is, you do not get ready first. You start first, and readiness comes after.

Every day you delay, you remain stuck where you are. Every day you take action, even small action, you move closer to the stronger, healthier version of yourself.

The Real Reason to Start

Working out is not just about losing weight or gaining muscle. It is about taking back control of your life. When you train your body, you train your mindset. You teach yourself that you can do hard things, stay committed, and push past limits you once believed were fixed.

Fitness is about building confidence from the inside out. It is the feeling of strength when you wake up, the energy throughout your day, and the pride of knowing you are doing something good for yourself.

You might start to look better, certainly, but you will feel better long before that. Your mood lifts, your focus sharpens, and your stress drops. Movement heals more than just your body. It also clears your head.

Exercise releases endorphins, the body's natural mood elevators. It reduces cortisol, the stress hormone that wreaks havoc on your health. Regular movement improves sleep quality, boosts immune function, and enhances cognitive performance.

These benefits begin immediately, not after you lose 20 pounds or complete a program, but after your very first workout. The physical transformation is just the surface. Underneath, you are rewiring your brain, strengthening your heart, and building resilience. You are proving to yourself that you have agency over your health and your future. That realization alone is powerful enough to change everything.

The Power of Momentum

Starting today does not mean you have to commit fully overnight. It just means you do something: walk, stretch, lift, breathe. Action builds momentum, and momentum builds habits.

The hardest part is showing up. Once you do, everything else becomes **easier**. Five minutes turns into fifteen. One workout turns into three. One healthy meal turns into a week of better choices.

Do not overthink it. Just move. The body follows the mind, but the mind gets stronger when you act.

You do not need to be fit to start. You start to get fit.

Momentum is a psychological force as much as a physical one. When you complete one small task, your brain registers success and becomes more willing to attempt the next. This is why starting, no matter how small, is so critical.

Each action you take builds evidence that you are someone who follows through. Over time, this identity shift becomes your greatest asset. You stop seeing yourself as someone who "should" work out and start seeing yourself as someone who does. That shift in identity makes consistency effortless because you are no longer fighting against who you think you are.

Excuses vs. Progress

Everyone has reasons not to start: no time, too tired, too old, too busy. However, those same excuses will still be there next week, next month, and next year. What changes is you—if you choose to change.

You will never regret a workout, but you will always regret not taking care of yourself sooner. You do not need perfect conditions. You just need willingness.

Even a small workout done consistently will outperform a "perfect plan" that never begins.

Excuses are often fear disguised as logic. Fear of failure, fear of discomfort, fear of judgment. But here is the truth: the discomfort of starting is temporary, while the discomfort of staying unhealthy is permanent. Every excuse you accept today becomes harder to overcome tomorrow.

Time does not create better circumstances. It creates regret. The best time to start was years ago. The second-best time is right now. You have more time than you think; you simply need to prioritize differently. Thirty minutes is less than 2% of your day. You can find it if you truly want to.

The Gift of Movement

Your body is built to move. Every muscle, every joint, every breath you take is a reminder that movement is a gift, not a chore. Do not take it for granted. It's always helpful to remember that there are people who wish they could do what you can. So while you have the ability, use it. Strength is a blessing, and it grows when you work it.

Start Simple, Start Now

Today could be the day you draw a line and say, "I am done waiting."

You do not need a gym membership, supplements, or fancy shoes. You just need the decision to start.

Here is your first challenge:

- Move for 10 minutes today
- Drink a full glass of water
- Write down one reason you want to get stronger

That is it. You have already started.

Every rep, every walk, every good choice adds up. The key is consistency, not **perfection**. If you start today, a month from now, you will be proud you **did**. A year from now, you will be unrecognizable in strength, in mindset, and in confidence.

Do not wait for motivation. Do not wait for Monday. Do not wait for anyone to tell you it is time. Start now. Your future self will thank you. The person you will become is watching you right now, hoping you make the choice to begin. Every day you delay is another day that the future version of yourself has to wait. Make the decision. Take the first step. Everything else will follow.

Chapter 3
When to Train:
Building Your Routine

One of the most common questions beginners ask is, "When is the best time to work out?" The truth is, the best time is the time you will actually show up.

There is no magic hour that guarantees better results. Morning, afternoon, or night; each has its benefits. What matters most is consistency. Your body adapts to what you do often, not what you do once in a while.

Morning Training

Working out early sets the tone for your day. You complete it before distractions arise, your energy stays higher, and you build discipline right from the start. For many people, it is easier to maintain because there is less chance of plans interfering.

If you are not a morning person, it might take a week or two to adjust. Start small, with perhaps 20-30 minutes. Once you experience how good it feels to start your day strong, it becomes easier to maintain.

Morning workouts also capitalize on willpower, which is highest early in the day. Before your mind gets cluttered with decisions and stress, you complete your most important task. This creates a sense of accomplishment that carries through your entire day.

Additionally, morning exercise can regulate your circadian rhythm, improving sleep quality at night. Many people find that morning training increases their overall productivity because physical activity enhances mental clarity and focus.

If you struggle with morning workouts, try preparing everything the night before. Lay out your clothes, set your alarm across the room, and remove all friction. Your morning self will appreciate the planning.

Evening Training

Evening workouts can be excellent as well. They help relieve stress after a long day, and your body is already warm and fueled from meals. You might even feel stronger lifting later in the day.

Just ensure your workouts do not interfere with your sleep. If you train late, give yourself time to wind down. Stretch, breathe, and relax before bed.

Evening training allows you to release the stress accumulated throughout the day. Physical exertion becomes a form of meditation, clearing your mind and resetting your nervous system.

Your body temperature is also naturally higher in the late afternoon and early evening, which can improve performance and reduce injury risk. Your muscles are more flexible, and your reaction time is sharper.

For people with demanding mornings or family obligations, evening workouts offer a practical solution. The key is to avoid intense exercise within two hours of bedtime, as it can elevate cortisol and make falling asleep difficult. If evenings work best for you, embrace them fully and make that time sacred.

Consistency Beats Timing

Some days you will have energy; some days you will not. That is normal. The goal is not to be perfect but to be present. Even if you do not feel like it, show up and do something. Momentum is built through repetition, not inspiration.

Whether you train in the morning, on your lunch break, or after work, try to keep your time slot consistent. Your body responds well to routine, helping build a habit and keep progress steady.

There is no perfect time, just a consistent one.

Building a Weekly Routine

If you are new to training, start with three days per week. That is sufficient to see progress without burning out. A simple structure looks like this:

- **Day 1:** Full-body strength or resistance training
- **Day 2:** Rest, walk, or stretch
- **Day 3:** Cardio or mobility work
- **Day 4:** Rest or light activity
- **Day 5:** Strength training again
- **Day 6:** Optional active day (walk, hike, play sports)
- **Day 7:** Rest

Keep it flexible. Remember, life happens. If you miss a day, do not quit; just pick up where you left off. The key is getting back on track quickly.

This weekly structure balances work and recovery, preventing both burnout and stagnation. As you adapt, you can gradually increase the frequency or intensity. The principle of progressive overload, gradually increasing stress on your body, is what drives improvement.

However, progress is not linear. Some weeks you will feel strong; others you will struggle. That is normal and expected.

Your routine should serve your life, not control it. Flexibility within structure is the sweet spot. Honor your commitments when possible, but extend grace to yourself when life intervenes. What matters is the overall pattern, not individual days. Consistency over weeks and months trumps perfection on any single day.

Rest Is Part of Training

Rest days are not "lazy" days, but they are when your muscles actually grow and your body resets. Without recovery, you will feel sluggish and risk injury. Sleep well, stretch, hydrate, and move lightly on off days.

Recovery is not the opposite of progress; it is part of it.

Your Time, Your Rules

The best routine is one that fits your lifestyle, not one that forces you into someone else's schedule. Start with what you can handle and build from there.

You do not need hours each day. You just need intention and consistency.

Find your rhythm and stay consistent. That is the foundation of lasting progress. Your schedule should reflect your priorities and constraints. If you have young children, train during nap time or after bedtime. If you work irregular hours, keep your workout short and mobile-friendly.

The point is to design a system that works for you, not against you. When your routine aligns with your reality, adherence becomes natural. Stop comparing your journey to others. Their schedule, responsibilities, and circumstances differ from yours. What matters is that you find your sustainable path forward.

Chapter 4
Where to Start:
Movement Basics

You do not need fancy equipment or a gym membership to start your fitness journey. What you need is a foundation: a few simple movements that train your body to get stronger, move better, and stay balanced.

The best place to begin is with bodyweight exercises. They teach control, build coordination, and prepare your joints and muscles for heavier work later on.

The Five Basic Movements

All exercises derive from five main movement patterns. Learn these, and you can build any workout you will ever need.

1. **Push:** Exercises where you press weight away from your body
- Examples: Push-ups, shoulder presses, dips
- Builds chest, shoulders, and triceps

2. **Pull:** Movements where you bring resistance toward your body
- Examples: Rows, pull-ups, resistance band pulls
- Strengthens your back and biceps

3. **Squat:** Any exercise where you bend your knees and lower your body
- Examples: Bodyweight squats, goblet squats
- Builds legs, glutes, and core stability

4. **Hinge:** Movements where you bend at the hips while keeping your spine straight
- Examples: Deadlifts, hip thrusts, kettlebell swings
- Strengthens hamstrings, glutes, and lower back
5. **Core:** Movements that train your midsection to stabilize your body
- Examples: Planks, mountain climbers, leg raises
- Builds strength that supports everything else

Every workout you do will include some combination of these five. Mastering the basics will make you strong, confident, and injury-resistant.

These movement patterns mirror how your body naturally functions in daily life. Pushing opens doors and lifts objects overhead. Pulling brings things toward you and helps you climb. Squatting allows you to sit and stand. Hinging lets you pick things up from the ground safely. Core stability protects your spine during all movement.

When you train these patterns, you are teaching your body to move efficiently in the real world. This functional approach reduces injury risk and improves quality of life. Athletes train these patterns. Manual laborers use them daily. They are universal, timeless, and essential. Master them, and you master movement itself.

How to Start

Begin with short, full-body workouts two or three times per week. Focus on form over speed, because after all, you are teaching your body how to move efficiently.

Here is a simple sample routine to get started:

Beginner Full-Body Routine (3x per week):

- Bodyweight Squats: 3 sets of 10–12
- Push-ups (or knee push-ups): 3 sets of 8–10
- Dumbbell or Band Rows: 3 sets of 10
- Glute Bridges: 3 sets of 12
- Plank: 3 rounds of 20–30 seconds

Rest 30–60 seconds between sets. Move slowly and breathe through each rep. You do not need to chase exhaustion. You are building skill and strength.

This routine covers all five movement patterns in under 30 minutes. It requires minimal equipment and can be done anywhere. The beauty of full-body workouts is efficiency. You train everything in one session, maximizing results while minimizing time.

As you progress, you can add weight, increase repetitions, or reduce rest periods. The workout might feel easy at first. That is intentional. You are grooving movement patterns into your nervous system, building a foundation that will support heavier loads later.

Rushing this phase leads to injury and poor form habits. Be patient. Master the basics. Your future self will thank you for the solid foundation.

Progress Over Perfection

Do not worry about how much weight you can lift or how many reps you can do. Worry about getting better every week, even if a little. That might mean one more rep, one better push-up, or just showing up on a rough day.

Small improvements done consistently equal big results over time.

Keep It Safe

Good form matters more than heavy weight. Listen to your body. If something hurts (not soreness, but pain), adjust or stop. Stretch before and after workouts and stay hydrated. Your body will thank you.

Pain is your body's warning system, and therefore, ignoring it invites injury. Soreness is normal; sharp or shooting pain is not. Learn the difference. If an exercise causes pain, modify it or substitute it with something else. There is always an alternative.

Additionally, remember that proper warm-ups prepare your body for work by increasing blood flow and joint mobility. Spend five minutes walking, doing arm circles, or performing light versions of your working exercises. Cool-downs help transition your body back to rest and reduce muscle stiffness.

Stretching improves flexibility and aids recovery. Hydration supports every bodily function, from muscle contraction to waste removal. These basics, which include proper form, adequate hydration, and smart programming, are not optional. They are the difference between sustainable progress and preventable injury.

The Takeaway

Fitness starts with movement, not heavy lifts or fancy equipment. When you master the basics, everything else becomes easier.

Start simple, move well, and stay consistent. The strength you build here will carry you to the next level of your journey. These fundamental movements are not a phase to rush through, but they are skills to refine continuously.

Even advanced athletes return to basics regularly because fundamentals never stop mattering. Strength is built on a foundation of solid movement patterns. Speed, power, and endurance all depend on the quality of your basic mechanics. Respect the process. Trust the simplicity. The basics work.

Chapter 5
Staying Consistent:
The Real Secret

Motivation gets you started. Consistency keeps you going.

Every goal, whether it is losing weight, building muscle, or feeling better, comes down to one thing: showing up, even when you do not feel like it.

Why Consistency Matters

Your body adapts through repetition. The more consistent you are, the faster your results come. Skipping a workout does not ruin progress, but giving up after one missed day does.

Discipline beats motivation every time.

Consistency is the compound interest of fitness. Small deposits made regularly grow exponentially over time. One workout changes nothing. One hundred workouts change everything. Your body does not respond to what you do occasionally. Instead, it responds to what you do habitually. This is why weekend warriors often struggle with results despite intense effort. Their bodies never adapt because the stimulus is inconsistent.

Meanwhile, someone doing moderate workouts three times weekly sees steady progress because their body recognizes the pattern and responds. Adaptation requires predictability. Your muscles grow when they consistently face resistance. Your cardiovascular system improves when regularly challenged. Your nervous system sharpens when repeatedly practicing movement patterns.

Consistency creates the environment for transformation.

Build the Habit

Start small. If you cannot do an hour, do 20 minutes. If you cannot train five days a week, train three.

Once movement becomes routine, it is no longer something you "have to do"; it is just part of your day.

Tips to stay on track:

- Schedule your workouts like appointments
- Lay out your clothes or pack your gym bag the night before
- Track your sessions, even briefly; it builds accountability
- Surround yourself with people who support your goals

Habits form through repetition in consistent contexts. If you always train at the same time and place, your brain begins to associate that context with exercise. Eventually, the behavior becomes automatic. This is why routine is so powerful: because it removes the need for motivation. You just do it because it is what you do at that time.

Identity also plays a role. If you see yourself as "someone who works out," you will act accordingly. Protect your new identity by honoring your commitments.

Each time you follow through, you reinforce the belief that you are disciplined and capable. Each time you skip unnecessarily, you weaken that belief. Treat your workouts as non-negotiable appointments with yourself. You would not cancel on your boss or your child. Do not cancel on yourself either.

Progress Over Perfection

Some days you will crush your workout. Other days, just getting through it is a win. Both matter. Do not chase perfection, chase progress.

Progress looks like:

- Lifting a little more
- Moving with better form
- Recovering faster
- Feeling stronger mentally and physically

When Life Gets in the Way

Life will get busy. You will have stress, work, family, and days where fitness feels impossible. That is normal.

Do what you can with what you have. Even a walk counts. Movement is medicine, so use it to reset, not punish yourself.

On difficult days, lower your standards but never your commitment. If a full workout feels impossible, do half. If half is too much, do ten minutes. If ten minutes is beyond reach, stretch for five. The specific workout matters less than maintaining the habit. You are teaching yourself to show up regardless of circumstances. This resilience transfers to every area of life.

When you prove you can handle discomfort and still take action, you build mental toughness that serves you in work, relationships, and adversity. Fitness goes beyond physical training because it is also character development. The person who trains when tired, stressed, or unmotivated is building something deeper than muscle. They are building an unshakeable sense of self.

The Takeaway

Many think consistency is about never missing. Truth be told, it is about never quitting.

Keep showing up, one day at a time. Over weeks and months, those small efforts compound into real change. Stay patient. Stay steady. The results will come. Trust the process even when progress feels invisible.

Trees do not grow visibly day-to-day, yet they become mighty over years. You are the same. Every workout is a deposit into your future self. Stay consistent, and time will reveal the transformation.

Chapter 6
Mindset & Motivation:
Training the Inner Game

Your body follows your mind. If your mindset is not right, your workouts will not stick. Fitness is not just physical. In fact, it is mental first.

Why Mindset Matters

The way you think shapes the way you train. When you see workouts as punishment, you will avoid them. When you see them as an investment, you will crave them.

Shift your focus from "I have to work out" (obligation) to "I get to move" (opportunity). Every rep is a chance to get better, not a chore to check off.

Your mindset determines your ceiling. Two people can follow the same program, but the one with the stronger mindset will achieve better results. Why? Because mindset influences effort, consistency, and resilience. When you believe training is important, you prioritize it. When you see it as optional, you skip it. Your beliefs become self-fulfilling prophecies.

If you think you are not athletic, you will not push yourself. If you believe you are capable, you will find a way. This is why mindset work is as important as physical training. You must actively cultivate empowering beliefs.

Motivation vs. Discipline

Motivation fades. Discipline lasts.

There will be days you do not feel like moving. That is when your discipline kicks in; when you train your mind to act, not negotiate.

How to stay driven:

- Set small, clear goals (Example: "I will work out three times this week")
- Track progress; seeing improvement builds momentum
- Celebrate effort, not just results
- Remember your "why" (health, strength, confidence); whatever drives you, remind yourself often

Motivation is an emotion that is both fleeting and unreliable. On the other hand, discipline is a skill that is built through practice and repetition. When you rely on motivation, you are at the mercy of your feelings. When you cultivate discipline, you act regardless of how you feel.

This distinction is critical. Motivated people start. Disciplined people finish. Motivation gets you to the gym once. Discipline gets you there 100 times. The good news is that discipline can be trained like any other skill. Every time you act despite not wanting to, you strengthen your discipline. Every time you honor a commitment to yourself, you build trust in your ability to follow through. Over time, discipline becomes your default mode. You stop debating whether to work out, and you just do it because that is who you are.

Train Your Mind Like You Train Your Body

Your thoughts are reps too. The more you practice positive self-talk, the stronger your mindset becomes.

Challenge negative self-talk. Replace "I cannot" with "I am learning." Replace "This is too hard" with "This is making me stronger." Your inner dialogue shapes your reality. Choose it carefully.

Progress is built through persistence, not perfection.

The Power of Patience

Results take time. You did not get out of shape overnight, and you will not transform overnight either. Be patient with your journey. Every small win, even showing up, eating better, and sleeping well, adds up. Mindset is the muscle that drives all others. Strengthen it daily.

Impatience kills more fitness journeys than lack of effort. People expect dramatic changes in weeks, then quit when reality does not match expectations. The truth is that meaningful transformation takes months and years, not days and weeks.

Your body changes slowly because it prioritizes survival over aesthetics. Rapid changes signal danger, triggering protective mechanisms that resist further change. Slow, steady progress signals safety, allowing sustainable adaptation. Embrace this reality. Celebrate process over outcomes. Did you show up consistently this week? That is a win. Did you improve your form? That is progress. Did you choose a healthy meal when tempted? That is growth.

These small victories matter more than the number on the scale because they represent the person you are becoming. Trust that if you focus on behaviors, results will follow.

The Takeaway

Your mental fitness determines your physical fitness. When you believe in your ability to improve, you will.

Train your body, but never forget to train your mind, because it's what carries you through when motivation runs out. The strongest muscle in your body is your mind. Develop it with the same intensity you apply to your physical training. Read, reflect, and refine your thoughts. Your mindset is your ultimate competitive advantage.

Chapter 7
Staying in the Game: Longevity & Lifestyle

Fitness is not a 30-day challenge. It is a lifetime commitment to taking care of your body. The goal is not perfection but sustainability.

Think Long-Term

Working out may make you look good, but it is also a lot about feeling good, moving well, and staying active as you age.

You want strength that carries you through life: climbing stairs with ease, playing with your children, staying independent, and feeling confident in your body. Remember that you are not training for today; you are training for every tomorrow.

Longevity is about preserving function, not just appearance. As you age, muscle mass naturally declines—a process called sarcopenia. Without resistance training, you lose approximately 3-8% of muscle mass per decade after 30. This loss accelerates after 60, leading to frailty, falls, and loss of independence. However, strength training reverses this decline at any age.

Studies show people in their 70s and 80s can build significant muscle and strength with proper training. The person who maintains strength maintains autonomy. They live independently longer, recover from illness faster, and enjoy a higher quality of life. Every rep you do today is insurance for your future. You are building resilience against aging.

Build Habits, Not Phases

Short-term programs can jump-start progress, but long-term results come from daily habits.

Focus on these fundamentals:

- Move daily; walk, stretch, or train
- Eat whole foods most of the time
- Sleep enough; your body repairs during rest
- Manage stress; breathe, journal, or meditate
- Stay consistent; if you miss a day, get back to it

Habits are the compound interest of self-improvement. A single workout has minimal impact. Ten thousand workouts create a completely different person. The transformation happens so gradually you barely notice it day-to-day, yet over years the change is profound. This is why systems matter more than goals.

Goals are destinations; systems are the vehicles that get you there. Instead of focusing on losing 20 pounds, focus on the habits that naturally lead to weight loss. Instead of targeting a specific physique, focus on training consistently. The habits you build today determine who you become tomorrow. Make them non-negotiable. Protect them fiercely. Your future depends on them.

Adapt as You Grow

Your fitness needs will change. What worked at 25 might not fit at 45, and that is completely normal and acceptable. You can always adjust your training, recovery, and nutrition to match your body's needs.

Longevity comes from listening, not forcing.

Adaptability is a survival skill. Your body changes constantly; for instance, hormones shift, metabolism adjusts, injuries occur, and life circumstances evolve. Rigid adherence to a single approach guarantees eventual failure.

The person who thrives in the long term learns to adapt. If heavy squats no longer feel good, switch to lunges. If high-intensity cardio leaves you feeling fatigued, try lower-intensity options.

Flexibility within your fitness practice ensures sustainability. This also applies to life seasons. New parents have different time constraints than retirees. People with demanding careers need different recovery protocols than students. Honor where you are right now rather than clinging to what worked in the past. Adaptation may feel like weakness at times, but it is wisdom. The strongest trees bend in the wind rather than breaking.

Keep Learning

Stay curious about health and movement. Try new activities: boxing, yoga, hiking, and swimming. Keeping things fresh prevents burnout and helps you stay motivated.

Fitness should add to your life, not control it.

Variety serves multiple purposes. Physically, different activities challenge your body in unique ways, preventing adaptation plateaus and reducing the risk of overuse injuries. A runner who adds swimming develops upper-body strength while giving their joints a break. A lifter who tries yoga improves flexibility and balance.

Mentally, variety keeps training interesting. Boredom is a silent killer of consistency. When training feels like a chore, you will eventually quit. But when you genuinely enjoy movement, it becomes something you look forward to rather than endure. Explore different modalities. Find what resonates with you.

Fitness is a vast landscape, so do not limit yourself to one corner of it. The person who enjoys their training is the person who sustains it for life.

The Takeaway

Longevity is built on consistency, balance, and self-awareness. Take care of your body now, and it will take care of you later.

Keep showing up, not for a deadline, but for a lifestyle.

Stay strong. Stay moving. Stay in the game. Remember that fitness is not a destination you reach and then abandon. It is a practice you commit to for life. The strongest 80-year-olds are not people who trained hard in their youth and then stopped, but the ones who never stopped.

Consistency across decades creates extraordinary results. Start building that consistency today, and 30 years from now, you will still be moving with strength, confidence, and vitality while others struggle with basic activities.

Conclusion:
Keep It Simple, Keep Going

You now have everything you need to begin your journey: basic knowledge, structure, and the right mindset. From understanding how your body moves to fueling it with real food and staying consistent, every small step matters.

The most important thing to remember is this: do not stop.

Even when progress feels slow, you are still moving forward. Every rep, every healthy meal, every good night's sleep; it all compounds into lasting change. You do not need to do it all at once. Just start.

Build momentum one day at a time. Stay patient with yourself. Trust the process. The person you are becoming is worth every effort you are putting in today.

The transformation you seek will not happen overnight, and that is perfectly acceptable. Real change is built in the unsexy middle: the days when no one is watching, when results feel invisible, when showing up feels pointless. Those are the days that define you. Those are the days that separate people who transform from people who try to quit.

You will face obstacles. You will have setbacks. You will question whether it is worth it. In those moments, remember why you started. Remember that every single person who achieved the fitness you desire went through the same struggles. The only difference is that they kept going.

You have been given one body for this entire life. Treat it with respect. Move it with purpose. Fuel it with intention. Rest it with care. This is about honoring the gift of physical capability while you have it.

Strength fades if not maintained. Health deteriorates if not protected. But with consistent effort, you can thrive at any age and any stage.

The principles in this book are simple, but simple does not mean easy. Application requires discipline, patience, and unwavering commitment to yourself. Some days will be harder than others. Push through anyway. Some weeks, you will feel stuck. Keep showing up anyway.

Progress is not linear. You will have breakthroughs and plateaus, victories and setbacks. All of it is part of the journey. What matters is that you stay in the game.

Five years from now, you will either wish you had started today, or you will be grateful that you did.

Choose gratitude. Choose action. Choose yourself.

Your future is built by what you do today. Make it count.

Welcome to the rest of your life. Make it strong.

Made in the USA
Coppell, TX
18 January 2026